Contents

What's awake?

Some animals are awake when you go to sleep.

Animals that stay awake at night are **nocturnal**.

Rats are awake at night.

What are rats?

Rats are **mammals**.

Mammals have **fur**.

Mammals live with their babies.

Mammal babies drink milk from their mother's body.

What do rats look like?

snout

tail

Rats look like big mice with long tails.

They have dark eyes and pointy **snouts**.

A rat's **fur** can be brown or black.

It can be grey or white.

Where do rats live?

Rats live together in **nests**.

In the wild, they live in trees or underground.

In cities, some rats live in old buildings.

Some live in underground pipes.

What do rats do at night?

Rats wake up after dark.

They leave their **nest**.

Rats look for food.

They can eat all night.

What do rats eat?

Rats eat almost anything.

In the wild, rats eat eggs,
bugs and plants.

In the city, rats also eat rubbish.

They eat food people leave out
for their pets.

What do rats sound like?

Rats can squeak and whistle.

They can also make a chirping noise.

How are rats special?

Rats have very strong teeth.

This rat is chewing on a deer **antler**.

Rats' front teeth do not
stop growing.

They need to chew things to
keep their teeth short.

Where do rats go during the day?

Rats go back to their **nest** during the day.

They may also look for food during the day.

They take care of their babies.

Then they sleep for most of the day.

Rat map

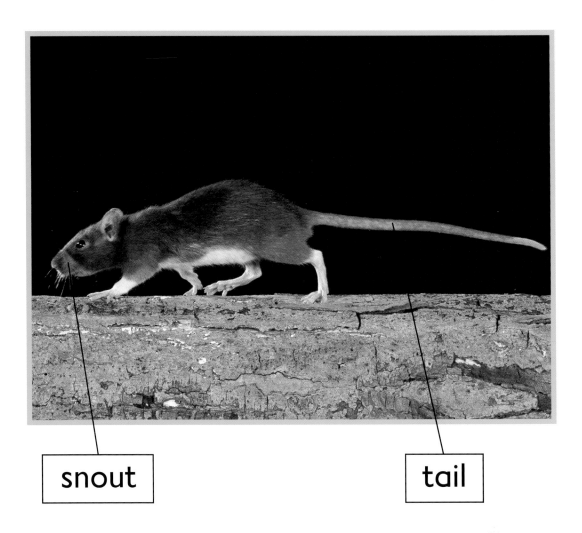

snout

tail

Glossary

antler
hard part that some animals have growing on their head

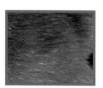

fur
short, soft hair

mammal
animal that is covered in fur and feeds its babies with milk from its own body

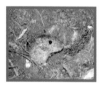

nest
home that birds and some animals make

nocturnal
awake at night

snout
the long nose and mouth that some animals have

Index